When We're Awake At Night

When We're Awake At Night

Cover art by Indika Roseler

Levi Laws

Published by Tablo

Table of Contents

For Linda,
I hope you're proud lovely.

trigger warning

As this is a discussion about mental health, some of these poems could be a bit unsettling or upsetting. It is not my intention to send anyone down a negative path, quite the opposite. A clear reading of the whole book will show that. Many people experience these situations, feelings, and life events that end up being suppressed. My goal is only to show my journey. These emotions are real, these emotions are valid.

Preface

Mental health is an increasingly talked about topic, and for good reason. Roughly 17.2 million adults in the United States have experienced some sort of major depressive disorder in 2019 alone. Considering the negative stigmas associated with discussing mental health, having depression, or anxiety, or any mental health disorder in general, it is safe to assume the amount of unreported cases would boost that number astronomically.

Suicide was the 10th leading cause of death in 2019, and that number has grown every year. It is the second leading cause of deaths for ages 10-34, and the 4th leading cause of death for ages 35-54. My home state of Oregon, is in the top third of suicide rates in the United states. Men have died 3.6x more to suicide than women, and a lot of that can be due to toxic masculinity seeping into the consciousness of men and therefore being seen as "weak" for getting help. However, women experience depression at roughly twice the amount as men between the ages of 14-18. This is a disorder that does not care about your sex.

Additionally. a disorder sort of synonymous with depressive disorder is clinical anxiety. Anxiety disorders are the most common mental illnesses, affecting over 40 million Americans each year. 9.9 million adults have reported having a panic attack in the last year.

These are issues that allow for many people to be wrongfully looked down upon for being weak and broken. Many are looked down upon for attempting to get better, whether that be by medication, or therapy. People often struggle to overcome these stigmas, and the recovery process becomes stifled because of it.

Tearing each other down in our weakest moments does no one any good. Learning how to love, support, and be there for someone affected by one of these dreadful disorders rather than patronizing or even worse, feeling disdain for them is what we need to move towards. Education is the best power, and the more we educate ourselves on these topics, the better we can support the ones closest to us who struggle with these disorders. We are all someones brother, sister, daughter, son, grandson, etc. It is time to destigmatize the discussion around mental health.

This book is a many things, but it is mainly a long story of a journey through mental health. Breakdown, recovery, relapse, and everything that goes into the mental health journey from my perspective. All of the untold moments we spend awake at night fighting to stay. All of the moments spent reflecting in pain about times our disorders have held us back. All of the moments of feeling like we did not belong. All of the moments of weakness. All of the moments of strength. I did my best to illustrate just what it feels like to experience these moments.

To those still stigmatizing mental health, I hope this opens your eyes a touch. I hope whoever reads this takes even the slightest bit of comfort in knowing they aren't alone, and there is light at the end of the tunnel, and if anyone hasn't told you today:
I love you, and you're worth the fight.

Thank you for listening,

-Levi

What...?

What is the point without passion?
Days become restless, nights become endless.

What is the point without love?
The void grows, never was it protected.

What is the point without friendship?
Together alone, stuck in our jail cell.

What is the point without trust?
Suspicion weighing down like a barbell.

What is the point of giving up,
if you still have the passion?

Why??

Why am I here?

Why can't I think?

Why can't I write?

Why can't I blink?

Why am I paralyzed?

Can't breath or speak

Why am I like this?

Is something wrong with me?

Why am I weak, broken, and bruised?

Why do I feel taken and used?

I was fine minutes ago,

and now I can't move.

Why won't this end?

It's lasting eternally.

Am I the cause of all of my suffering?

Why am I here?

Where did I go?

Its over now,
and I'm still alone.

Comparison

Was I wrong?
I sit here pondering fatal feelings.
Am I weak?

The feeling is never ending.
Collapsing into myself until sweet solace of slumber separates
me.
Was she right?

She must have chose him for some reason.
The biggest fear creeps into the crevices of my consciousness.

Why am *I* not enough?

Insomnia

The night draws close, calling out to me with its luminous soul.
What should be the end is now the beginning.
Fleeting memories try and destroy the calm.
Black is the ink.
Black is the pen.
Black is the desk.
As is the mind.
As is the heart.
As is the soul.
When the light breaks, the heart follows.
The calm is no more.

Powerless

An empty shell of what I built.
No vehemence.
No desire.
No ambition.
No fire.
How did you manage it like it was nothing?
Seemingly endless satisfaction turned into seemingly endless
suffering.

A Trip to Another Dimension

I bought the biggest mirror I could find.
I set it against my wall, stood back and stared.
Disheveled I looked as my mind began its usual incineration of
my body, until my glance changed to my eyes.
Staring for so long real life began to fade.

I felt a cold wood under my feet.
A brisk morning breeze
sent a comforting chill down my spine.
This is an unrecognizable satisfaction.

Peering up to a front yard, with a rusted old fence.
My children ran past chasing each other.
Their laughs levitated into the air, filling it
with the simplest joy I have never experienced.

You came up behind me and touched my arm,
laying your soft cheek on my shoulder.
The scent of rose perfume filled my senses
as we peered out into this new reality.

My glance snapped back to my broken gaze.
Face now flushed, my eyes began to fog.
This reality is inconceivable
This reality is never real.

Remembering

I picked you up at 1:30 p.m.
Watched you skip to my car to the beat of my heart.
Can it be like this forever?
I would eventually accept all your love for me as genuine as the
love a mother has for her child flaws and all, I thought as I
looked at you at the stoplight.
But how could someone like you love me?
How would I ever believe your reassurance was enough
insurance?
You turned back and smiled at me, and I decided to believe.
I cherished every moment that day,
and I dropped you off at 2 a.m. for the last time.

?

Each time you looked me in the eyes and told me you loved me,
I wonder if you felt the same pain I feel now, knowing you were
lying.

Would it have been so hard to just tell me the truth?

Insufficient Instructor

Brought here by the ones before me.
Unwavering desire to inspire.
Give back to what was given to me.
Each day, a moment to admire.

Each bell rung, each sheet passed.
Every moment spent,
listening to their laughs.
This is my destiny, where all time will be spent.

Sudden moments of disgrace,
did take it all away.
To never see their face,
To this affair made a heart decay.

Each day fought for triumphant return.
Sauntering nights of no reply.
A weary heart did ever yearn,
for sweet release of last goodbyes.

Shunned away to Hell's despair,
A moment of mercurial misery.
A perpetual nightmare.
I have failed the ones closest to me.

Alone

A monastic mindset manipulates my mind.
This is my new reality.

Staring at my ceiling, sequestered from my soul.
My sheets are binding to me.

There are no more thoughts that haven't been thought.
A cycle has situated itself in my
psyche of kisses, subtle touches.

Every red flag that you so beautifully
explained away that I bought without concern.
As a battered child in a toy store, mothers card in hand.

Solitude is where I should surrender,
but surrender is a sweet release that I am not ready for.

So for now leave me alone.

13

Over-saturated words said.
Munificent acts over and over again.
Wafting in the scents to remember.
Torridness becomes tortuous,
Kismet is purposeless.
Mellifluous music sours in place of silence.
Sedition seems to be the best compliance.

Immutable feelings are immortal.
Soliloquy's don't feel necessary; not anymore.

Tumultuously Trapped

I could never scream.
Anger was never to be shown to you.
Held in by fear and my self esteem.
How could I ever stand up to you?

Hold the upper hand,
Turn the other cheek
Take the higher ground.
Cliches to bottle your feelings inside me.

Men are supposed to scream
Isn't that what they tell us?
Be angry, be manly, be mean.
That's always the right thought process.

My father believed this was right,
and this is what I saw each day, more and more.
So why whenever voices sail to the sky,
do I get shaken to my very core?

That is what they teach us,
men are supposed to scream.
But no matter the lessons I have learned,
that can never be me.

Grin Truth

You tell your boy
to grow up and
then you wonder
why he has
stopped smiling.

A Prudent Promise

Shrieks of substance,
their siren song.
Crashes causing consciousness.
Gambits of grief
is our genesis.
I promise to protect you,
as the door begins
to decimate.
Tonight we suffer,
surrendering to strikes.
Blood red tears pass by
the faces of innocent.
One day, the promise
will be prudent.
But tonight we suffer,
together.

A Way to Feel

Purple ambiance stains my eyes.
Tracks of serotonin feel my ears, but evade my soul.
Yearning for release of what's inside.
Listening to The Devils call.

She's sharp; her persuasion is uncanny.
Avoiding her is unproductive.
The sensation of her in my fingers is necessary.
Twirling her metal in my fingers has become seductive.

We begin our delicate dance.
She leads me as she glides across her stage
Painting it immaculately with each collapse.
An art piece with the canvas perceived as deranged.

Slipping through my fingers, she falls to the floor.
Temporary thrilling escape from the numb.
The dance is over and I can't ignore,
the canvas is an over-painted one.

A Distance Often Traveled

Dropped into my seat with the same destination.
I begin my journey.
Music connects to my car
and begins to play softly and somberly.
I glance into the passenger seat,
coming to grips with a everlasting emptiness
that it seems to hold in moments like this.
Treacherously warm summer air
wafted away by subtle winds as
I move down the same road once again.
I hate this road.
Failure, shame and fearful familiarity
are what awaits me down this road.
Graying, decaying, thinning hair
is what awaits me down this road.
A sunset view of sinister silence
is what awaits me down this road.
And still I go.
This is the only way I know how to try
and make sense of this feeling.
I pass the cow that you would always point out
and now the void grows.
This isn't the road trip that I ever wanted,
but maybe the one I deserve.
So I still go.

Hey Dad

A life full of an
attempt to escape what
you represent. Abandoned at
your appeasement, never
given the slightest reason
for why another life was chosen.
Each mirror gaze is frozen with
the harsh reality that I can never
truly escape you. You left me with
your eyes, your voice, your smile.
So each good deed compiled to counter
each vile moment left unreconciled could
never allow for a even momentary escape.
Because each moment I gaze into that mirror
I hate what I see because of you.

Failed Responsibility

I often wonder
what you are
thinking about.
Once in awhile
I hope it is me.
To make up for
all the years
you never did.

Temporary Permanence

Press into the skin, fill me with love.
This is what will make me feel I'm enough.

The pain has grown to be rather splendid.
In fact, I dread each moment it's ended.

Smother ideas dreamed up in the mind.
Silence all critics who are nothing but blind.

The process is finished and the mirror reflects,
the thoughts in each instant will not interject.

Weeks pass when it saunters back into the front,
of my consciousness. I thought this was *done*.

But they'll never leave, no they'll never run.
So press into the skin, and fill me with love.

New Normal

I find myself back on this app once again.
A never-ending cycle we seem to go through.
The months pass when I find no luck.
Self esteem fades as quickly
as day to night in the Oregon winter.
This is never what I wanted.
I walk into my class and
see the pretty, quiet girl with tattoos
who, when she does speak,
sounds more intelligent than any professor.
Daydreaming about the confidence to just say a word.
Oh, if only to meet my forever person
not through a screen
but by "manning" up and speaking
even the simplest of sentences.
Running through a hundred scenarios
on how I could introduce myself.
Insecurities clutching me like a vise.
Time slips away, stealing my confidence
in its imminent end.
We are dismissed.
The day dream is over until next time.
Sauntered back to my room.
I open my phone,
and start swiping.

Minuscule Memories Make a Meek Man

I am sure you
probably forgot
about me long ago.
You told me the love you
had for me was fake.
But I still think about the first
compliment you ever gave me.
I wonder if any of it was real.
And now I always will with everyone.

Merciless Malevolence

You are self destructive.
You are addicting, and I can't stay away long.
You dig your ideology deeper into me with each click.
With each post.
With each scroll.
You are a merciless malevolence that controls us all.
And we obey, and we stay.
You are my distraction from everything,
even when I shouldn't be distracted by you.
You are self destructive,

Desiderare

Rolling around an unfamiliar town.
This became my home.

Lost in the light of your eyes.
daggers slid into my soul.

Re-patched.
Stitched.

Sewn back together as time cycled.
Pieced me back together, as a child a puzzle.

Your power was too much,
and this was proven to be so.

Now I roll around an unfamiliar town,
lost and alone.

A Nights Distraction, A Mornings Dissatisfaction

Is this love?
You sit at the edge of my bed, making small talk about my
tattoos.
Is this love?
Music plays in the background of my violet lit room.
Is this love?
Lips shackled sweetly, faces embedded effortlessly.
Is this love?
Collum grasped gamesomely.
Is this love?
Legs wrapped around me as a python its prey.
Is this love?
Eyes of a new soul where you used to lay.
Is this love?
A night turned to morning of a strangers descent.
Is this *love*?
It isn't you, so it could never be *it*.

Preparation

Goodbye could do it no justice,
maybe nothing said at all is better.
No, no distractions tonight; no numbness.
The reasons will follow in this treasure.

Relive the good, relive the bad.
Memories will be forgotten.
This an act more than grand.
This is where the change will blossom.

Tears do stroll as baby's in carriage.
This is no easy act at all.
But necessary is the carnage.
When the final curtain calls.

So let the tears mix with the ink.
A final memory in adoration.
The work is done, no more to think.
I have done my preparation.

Second Thoughts

You can always be there.
But lately I have trouble finding you.
My words become less articulate.
My diction less polished.
I have blocked you out.
Not some anymore, but all of you.
I never wanted to, but it is easier this way.
From yesterday,
to years ago,
you're slipping.
To finish the final act, I had to silence you.
The good and the bad.

One by One

One by one they all will fall.
Down the hatch, I take them all.

The sky is black and ever-glowing.
Time to seek the true unknowing.

Twist and pour till nothings left.
This is how I take your breath.

And one by one they all will fall,
so down the hatch I take them all.

Wires and Beeps

The trip was one of failure.

I don't want to be here.

Why am I here?

Wires and beeps, you all think this will help.

The night is never-ending.

Why didn't it work?

Let me go. Let me be free.

I had to come to acceptance they would not agree.

Play the game and you will be free.

The night was lonely.

Not a single visitor?

Not a single visitor.

I just want to go home, but I don't know where that is anymore.

My New Friend

They say this will help.
They say you're the best.
They say you will be the one to bring me out of this.

I feel so unsure.
I feel rather sick.
I sit in your lobby, and try to shake this itch.

You open your door and call out my name.
Your eyes are kind, and your smile is welcoming.
You let me believe for a second, that this will be the beginning.

Aftershock

Eyes averted in each entrance.
This is what I feel.
Disgust received in petulance.
To you, my feelings are not real.

Apprehension fills the air,
with door opening.
When will she snap, I can't bear,
the worry results in the sulking.

This is fake, is your go to jab.
You say to me always.
Pick yourself up by your bootstraps.
Men brush it of as dirt in the hallway.

Your ignorance is rarely bliss.
Hypocritical sentences spewed.
In your own head you seem to dismiss,
your own struggle you will exclude.

Drown them out in liquid courage.
This is how you will avoid,
experiencing your own discourage.
But screams to us will fill your void.

Change for you is unfeasible.
Kin of yours will defend.
The acts you do unrepeatable,
but each night said with shield in hand.

We are your burden, you will remind us.

Your life stolen away,
by children who feel disgust,
and nothing but surreal betray.

The time I am here you will remind,
me that my mind is broken.
This will last to the end of time,
even when words aren't spoken.

I wish for you to gain your sight.
Overcome with the reality,
This is a pointless fight.
I need to get away from your locality.

Fixing Broken Flowers

Time ticks, I run my hands
through the fibers of your couch
as the hair of the one I once loved.
Combing it, attempting to find comfort.
Open me up as the tulips in springtime.
Stepped on and mangled,
you attempt to repair them.
Stems rooted in soaked soil.
Leaves of love left on the ground.
Scared to bloom,
bested by beasts breaking down built barriers.
Your job is not an easy one.

Unseen Beauty

The most beautiful women,
I never truly knew.
Each gruesome night brimming,
with ways I could protect you.

Unhinged men utilizing terror,
as a way to keep you in.
Witnessing each lethal error,
tearing you limb from limb.

Watching time result in lacquer eyes,
begging for you to overcome.
If only the chance to revise,
but into demons you succumb.

Yearn to lay upon your chest,
listen to the solace voice.
Letting go of petulant pests.
Bask in love from your baby boy.

Casualty Weather

What is a journey without suffering?
What is a trip without you.

A captious mind now buffering.
This journey is a fluke.

It should've ended the first endeavor.
A man too feeble to endure.

They say this journey has casualty weather.
They know that is the true allure.

A Morning Out.

Prickly pasture beneath pale palms.
Dense denigration devours
an indisposed soul.

Acrimonious air allows for
wafting in wan wind and
exhaling in enmity with the environment.

Time to start the day.

Lovely

Letting go of you was implausible.
The experience still clear in my conscious after all these years.
My best friend; my only sense of soundness.
Letting go is out of the question.
I won't do it.
But you say I have no choice.
Exertion is strenuous. You need to let go.
Memories flood back as I walk into our sanctuary
where I once lay like a prince in your lap.
Now a bed of bleeding breaths takes its place.
With my best friend.
Ready to let go.
Approaching bedside, your eyes open,
Your beautiful lips curl into my favorite smile,
This is home.
As you grip my hand, I am transported to the past.
A past of the only childhood I hold fondly.
Sprinklers in the yard of your heavenly habitat.
Transcended tranquility.
Indescribable security.
A fog of a glazed gaze returns me.
No, this will not be so.
Who will take care of our tree??
Who will pillar every preposterous picture??
Who will give wonderment to needless writing??
Pointless questions when the real one stands.
Who else could ever love me unconditionally as you have?
When no one else did.
Your hand grips again and my gaze meets yours.
The suffering is salient in them.
A kiss upon the forehead.

A final *"I love you, lovely."*
Your hand slips out of mine.
And each night I slip back into reality.
Letting go of you was implausible.
So I never have, and I never will.

Dawns Displeasure

My nights are
littered with thinking
about the endless
ways I have
disappointed you.
But I know they
can never top the
dissatisfaction I have
given myself.

The Protective Devil

A giant in your mind of delusion.
Stomped into each "Safe space."
Tense air only results in confusion.
Why did we have to get sent to this place?

A Savior, you're held up to be.
Christened by your nails of moonshine.
Demons in your path of cleansing are we.
Punished for being alive.

The youngest receives his sentencing first.
Thin walls reveal to us all.
A sentence predictable; young Demon is worthless.
Punishment precedes of never leaving his halls.

Shouts and strikes to break his spirit.
The Devil hears the call.
"Save me from this saviors spewing.
Come please, save us all."

Shakes of buildings; none are safe,
when Devil faces Saviors demolition.
Protective of his protege.
A life will be the cost of admission.

Slashing and snarling between the two.
Sanguinary scenes avail.
No winner will be crowned tonight.
Between Heaven and Hell.

Enough to Frighten the savior away.

The Devil sits beside the bed,
of his demon protege.
Ichor wiped off of his head.

"We will survive the saviors storm."
Devil reassures this to him.
"Hidden Hypocrisy in her thorns.
Soon our lives will begin."

Strolled back through the decimation.
Devil returns to his purgatory.
Plotting their next destination.
Escape from the saviors dormitory.

Ambivalence

Where do I even begin to recover?
How can I repair something so seemingly desolate?
None of my questions will ever be answered.
Yet I continue to ask.
Ready to give up and give in
as each night turns into morning
and a mind cannot be rested.
Running down crepuscular crevices
with no shine in sight.
This voyage is desperate and ineffectual.
But you wont let me give in.
Not yet.
And as much as I love you,
I hate you for letting me suffer.
.

A Visit to My Future Home

A walk in night of brisk and brood,
did he stroll with credence.
Quaintly in the quixotic moon,
examining the grievance.

Anecdotes of thee by who he's lain hard by.
Noiseless neighbors await.
Fixed his eyes upon the Stygian sky.
This home is his escape.

There is no fix that will prevent,
his move in to this home.
No, there will be no chance to circumvent,
from where these bodies groan.

Why Am I Like This?

The embarrassment seems to haunt me each time I wake.
If only you knew that was never who I was.
I wonder if you ever will.

A Lifelong Fight

What have I become?
A child once engulfed in happiness.
A teen confused but pressing on.
An adolescent searching for his soul.
I was once just a boy, with countless endings.
Why can't I *want* to stay alive.

Momentary Measurement

This week I will believe your word,
kindly spoken, softly heard.

"You are enough," You stress to me.
"And soon the world *will* see."

I watch you analyze my thoughts.
You know the lies that I have bought.

Spent currency till none is left,
in those who have committed theft.

Stealing trust and self esteem,
with every little broken dream.

But you remind me of my worth,
So this week I will believe your word.

Foreboding Function

Encompassed by everyone,
I find myself.

Lost in this moment,
begging for help.

I want to leave,
but I can't move.

If everyone here knew,
that's when i'd lose.

Swallow the sentences,
imprisoned inside.

This moment will pass,
for now I will hide.

An Attempt to Breath

This Inhale is extensive.

I breathe in each time they told me they hated me without speaking.

Every time they screamed at me for being an inquisitive child.

Every time they told the lie that made me suppress myself.

Every time they made me question my love for my brothers.

Every time they reminded me my creativeness is wasteful.

Every time they made the man in the mirror seem desolate.

Every time they made me question myself as a man at all.

Every door slammed in my face.

Every broken window.

Everything a mess.

And I exhale.

Charity Case

Years of doubt has led
me to this very moment.
Surrounded by saddened souls.
Confined by companions,
or so I thought. How could one
whose ever called me their
 brother treat me with such disdain
in my lowest moments.
Ushered out in shame, as each
eye peered over to watch the show.
The facade is over, they know my worst
self, and never again can I escape the humiliation
when they try and return. Anger was never my taste,
but it's all that fills my soul when names of disgrace arise.

Moons come and go,
peering from a distance.
Longing for the moments
of before, craving coexistence.

Forced

The hostility I hold in my heart weighs heavier than all of the holy words you said would heal me.

To cure my crushed conscience requires more than counterfeit courage.

Summer Solstice

You remind me once again,
I am nothing but lazy.
My battle is not real.
"You are wasting away Get over it."

If it was ever that easy I would be free,
of every outburst you've ever had.
I sit and weigh my choices once
again: succumb, or fight back.

I have had enough of this tonight.
The execution ends today.
Lightning on a tree down my back,
as I stand and deliver my defenses.

You have lived as an incorrigible ignorant,
like a smoker on their last days.
Your smoking gun run out of ammunition.
As I lay before you the crimes you've committed.

You beg for me to leave, and once
accepted you beg for me to stay.
No argument will change your ways,
so I turn to experience uncertain freedom.

Your final blows will never leave the contents of my perception.
"She was right to leave, They all were.
You are a broken *man*. The word never less fitting.
An apologetic call from me is what she will receive."

A bag is packed, a door is slammed.

A brother left behind.
Rain pours past clouded cheeks,
A soul to be refined.

Sterile Soil

I have yanked
my roots from
the ground
without a pot
to place them.
But this is
already better
than the sterile
soil I was born in.

Goodbye For Now

A true savior in simpleton sheathe.
Where I stayed in uncertainty.

Soldiers of persecution,
by minds of delusion.

You had my back, and I yours.
We're here again, as rains of change pour.

Off to discover ourselves at last,
the tide has finally seemed to pass.

Much work will need be done.
But this work an ever necessary one.

Embrace that says we'll make it somehow,
But we must say goodbye for now.

Windfall

A trip to the town I will call home.
This is what I have always wanted.
A drive so sublime of trees and turns.
Thoughts racing as a Greyhound.
Pattering around my brain.
What to expect?
A pleasant unknown I could have never predicted.
This is my chance.
This is my dream.
This is my home.

Deserted Den

All I have ever
dreamed is all
I received.
Escape, education,
and the chance to be free.
So why when I sit
upon my new throne,
do I continue to feel
unconditionally alone.

Survivors Guilt

Trudging through the trenches,
We fought our destined fight.
We often took defenses,
when under fire in the night.

I led you through plunging fire.
I taught you tactics to survive.
In darkness I tried to inspire,
you to escape and thrive.

This war is one we did not request.
Thrust upon us by the "Gods."
So in you I have tried to invest,
in overcoming all the odds.

But plans did change upon sudden chance.
Now left on your own to fight.
With each letter that I glance,
in plea that you send at night.

I have escaped. I am now free.
The grips of war are gone.
But with each letter you send me.
I know the war is not won.

Admitted Amnesia

I forget love.
I forget trust.
I forget feelings
altogether.
I forget the past.
I forget my home.
But I hope
you will remember.

Cataclysmic Compensation

I run you.
I control your motives,
your thoughts,
your existence.
No matter what you have been told,
you depend on me.
Opportunities, friends, love.
You fear me.
I strain your nights
with second guessing.
You abhor me as the mind a drug,
and crave me just as much.
But why?
Escape is unattainable.
Succumb to me.
I have captured the souls of millions.
You are one, and you don't even know.
Then, when you think you have enough of me,
you never will.

A Friends Advice, A Minds Defiance.

You told me to go home today,
Look in the mirror and say, "I love you."

I promised you nothing would change.
Nothing seems to get through.

You implored me to just try.
I reluctantly whispered "okay."

But when faced with your task of trial,
I realized a lie can't be told today.

Grand Closing

The feeling is tactile, prying the lips apart.
What could ever be said, that has not been before?
Pause ensues, perspiration begins.
Trembling causes the closure.
Maybe they should never open again

Educations Trepidation

How did I get to the
point where I can't even
answer a question in
class before studying
stoic faces impressions
of me?
Listening to my voice
reverberate off walls,
focused on the sound
rather then the purpose.
My words become stumbled upon
each other as a drunk father into a room
of maltreated minors.
The rest of the day spent
picking apart pointless phrases.
This is torturous.
I think I won't speak anymore.

The Glitch

Being pleased with
ones self seems to
be the way to recovery.
So when will the
happiness of others
stop coming before
the well being of myself?

September Sunrise

Dreary Dusk turns to dominant dawn,
and not a moment of rest.
The morning shadows have spawned,
brisk air punches the chest.

Children return to school,
parents receive their break.
Morning coffee is brewed,
as dizzy fathers awake.

Breakfast is eaten,
together as routine.
A morning blissfully unbeaten.
A morning I've never seen.

These mornings are benumbed senses,
for children as we.
A new start with the same ending,
plays out on the screen.

A morning despondent,
as dense doors do shut.
A bus ride abundant,
I sit in the front.

Off to an escape,
that I've had before.
But once I return,
back through that dense door.

Be met with the hospice,
where I sit and I wait.
For here I am conscious
that my soul they abate.

Tragic Traditions

Traditions are tragic,
all stuck in routine.

Each year rather frantic,
each time we convene.

This time to be special,
this time to be bliss.

But each year they all revel,
in intoxicants kiss.

No memories made,
No love shown for truth.

All traditions fade,
when it controls you.

Confusion

Each day I
find myself
consumed by
finding someone
else. That is how
I tell myself I will
find myself. But the
only way to find myself seems
to be by finding no one else at all.

Treacherous Time Travel

Why some days does the idea of leaving my bed resemble the moment of stepping into all of the past?

When will I escape this?

22

Everyday I have to
convince myself to stay.
More so this time than ever.
Ascension of hopes.
Maybe I'll get a love, maybe a call,
maybe support, can I have
anything at all?
This day has become a burden.
An inconsistent array of emotions
I wish I never had to have.
A call out to anyone to prove me wrong.
Prove that what I want to convince
myself to do is not worth it.
Warmth.
Affection.
Compassion.
Support.
Love.
Please, please, please!
Anything! No?
That's okay. I am comforted knowing it
won't always be this way. A promise made
to a teenage self will come to fruition.
3 more years.
And when the day comes, all of the
warmth,
affection,
compassion,
support,
love,
will be called out in suffering shrieks.

Begged to be enough for my return.
But it won't be, and it never would be again.
But In my mind, those shouts would never
come, rather cheers of relief. I would like to
break the promise one day.
But for now it is sealed shut in
my own written fate.

Painful Progress

Each expressed feeling made
each moment uncomfortable.

But each pondered philosophy
allowed for momentary belief.

The trick now; how to make
each moment last a lifetime.

Moments of Regret

I think back on every essential mistake I made that lead me to
the moment I became who I am.
The moments I was slipping into my worst fears.
I could never be more sorry for those moments.
Clouded by cognition unconstructed, and you were left to deal.
The people I cared most for.
Accepting responsibility, it has to be time to get better.

The Forgotten One

A life to live,
you did not ask.

And so they give,
you your mask.

Struck down by those,
with drunkard domes.

With each great blow,
destroyed your home.

But through the time,
you did then rise.

Strong will and mind,
will be your prize.

The love I have,
will never fade.

I long to take,
your pain away.

I was not there,
when needed most.

Now haunted by,
a dreadful ghost.

Kept awake at night,
by pasts of cries-

of your painful plight,
and my demise.

Now seeing you fly,
is hearts release.

Go unwaveringly,
into your deserving peace.

Bud

A nickname always despised
by you. But each time
said with the purest form
of love I could ever give.
More pure than anything
I have given myself.
Each moment I stop
to see you grow I am
reminded just why I
need to be here.
Serene sky eyes full
of hope and a future
brighter than you can imagine.
The struggles each day aren't gone.
But the love for you will always outweigh them.

Maxamillion

The beautiful boy,
with soulful brown eyes.

You truly are,
a wonderful prize.

Each smile you give,
shines rather bright.

Each hug that you squeeze,
lights up all dark nights.

I see you and think,
of all that is left.

To leave now would be,
a hearts biggest theft.

So stay then I will,
and I'll watch you grow.

So big and so strong,
so far you will go.

The Boy Who Said Hi

A bell ringing, a moment
of true blissful freedom.
A bounce of a ball on warm
concrete echoes across the sky.

This court of escape I revel
in daily. Even when alone provides
the purest of pleasures.
My chance to express myself.

You came up, as shy as I
and kindly asked me to teach you.
Shocked by your friendship, I obliged.
And now I don't think I'd be here without you.

Thank you for saying hi.

Escaping Evanescence

Fearing the possibility of fading,
you tell me to be memorable.
Nightly acceleration of aging.
Your belief in me is admirable

The idea of making memories,
means the action of leaving sheltered
sanctuary. That just has never been me.
Too in love with the idea of being sequestered.

But you are right, once again
a change must be made.
I must overcome the strain,
of protection. This I can't evade.

I throw on my best clothes,
wander down the stairs neurotically.
Thrust open a thousand pound door,
Each moment measured methodically.

How will this world perceive me,
meaningless stares pierce through my soul.
But this change is necessary.
This is my journey to become whole.

Belief

And you said to me,
"It's okay to be broken,
because you can be fixed.
And you will be, with time."

Me, Myself, and I.

Today I took a moment,
to try and find my bliss.

The funny thing I noticed, is you
don't need to be there for it to exist.

Actually, no one does at all,
for me to love myself.

Today I was in awe,
to realize I don't need anyone else,

to be happy for a day,
to experience ecstasy.

Sometimes it okay,
to be only be with me.

Sheets of The Voiceless

I lost my ability to speak for myself for so long
I forgot how good it felt.
But what I have buried down for years
to protect you, tore me into a million pages of the
sheets I would express myself with.
I am ready to pick them up and put them together.

Change of Heart

A list of goodbye letters sat at home on my desk.
Today is only for hello.

Persistent Patience

It has taken years of patience,
to receive this feeling.
Nights of the mind pacing,
mornings spent reeling.

Conversations I had,
advice fought away each night.
Swinging like a nomad,
through each seasonal plight.

It feels good to be stationed,
in this euphoric moment.
I really hope that this patience
will never be stolen.

Reflection

Today is the first time I looked in the mirror and didn't see you, staring back at me reminding me you didn't choose me.

Today I saw myself, chose myself, smiled and moved on.

Liberating Letters

The thought of writing you to tell you I am okay and I hope you are too is an ever-present one.

Maybe it's best for us to both just be.

Meteoric Merriment

A day full of fortunate events,
and the best part was you.
Such an unexpected twist,
but for happiness i'll make do.

Accepted all flaws of my past,
open viewing of my scars.
The most comforting at last,
a kiss upon them in my car.

Moments of feeling enough,
scenes of flawless contentment.
I thought doing this would be tough,
but now I hope this will never end.

Accepting Adoration

How could life get
any better than this?

For so long I thought
i'd not escape depressions pits.

The question in the back of
my head: could this last?

For once, I think I will
let that question pass.

Inescapable Abyss

I felt your energy shift today.
I saw the hesitancy in your eyes, and felt the tenseness in your
soul. This secondhand strain I have felt over and over again.
To be followed with a message I have heard countless times,
you must go, I am not for you.
Suddenly all the scars you softly kissed away became tactile.
I wished to never be back here again.
I don't think I will ever escape.

Hallucinogenic Hours

Warm summer air hit fond faces, nuzzled in the comfort of your
hair.
Where had this been, and finally its mine.
Eyes closed.
Lips curled.
Tranquility transcended this moment.
Where did it go?
I've lost your sweet smell.
A sumptuous smile so salutary.
Was any of this existent?
I have started to forget if these feelings existed.

Back Again.

Maybe I wasn't as healed as I thought.
Because all the work I seemed to put in to get there,
was so easily taken away when you left.

This is the only time I have ever wished to be "manly",
maybe then I wouldn't feel as much.

Accepting Expiration

The ink has stopped flowing,
through my pen.

The petulant nights have stopped
turning into meaningful mornings.

The pages have stopped turning,
in my story.

I have given up,
This fight is unwinnable.

Piercing Eyes

Each time I pick up the cold metal release, your eyes all stare
back at me.
Watching as a I demolish my buildings, poisoned blood running
off your eyes onto my support beams.
I haven't been here in so long, but numb nights end in consistent
fights of my conscious.
So If this is what I have to do to feel anything at all, then I'm
okay with this momentary wrongness.

Realization

I sat at the park,
and stared at the spot.
Where I told my friend,
your lies that I bought.

I wonder about,
if I took it back,
and focused on me,
just where i'd be at.

It's clear to me now,
I'm nowhere near fixed.
I wonder If this,
is all that exists.

Just cycles of time,
of putting my worth,
in arms so devine
just to get hurt.

But thats all my fault,
so baby don't think,
that i'm blaming you.
This is on me.

I enter each moment,
delusionally convinced,
that this the answer,
to my minds pressing twitch.

But thats not the case,
no its never been.
It's constantly based,
off all of the men,

i've seen in my life.
What I hoped to avoid,
to try and use you,
to replace the void.

But you're no doctor,
or pill I can take.
For me to love you
a conscious needs to awake.

Mirror Man

I watched you grow old but never become older.
A leaf on a tree, falling fleetingly to the ground.
Swept away by wasteful winds.

Rumination

I don't know why I was ever scared about what I would find in the dark.

I stared up into its endless essence, and tonight found myself staring back.

Nightly reflections in the luminous sky have started to brighten my mind, and take me away from the substantial situation.

Why Escape the Inevitable?

A streetlight was surrounded
by majestic moths as I sat.
I watched them
clawing at the light.
Astounded that everyone
in darkness tries to escape it,
rather than learn from
it and embrace it.

Euphoric Epiphany

This time felt empty
for so long.

It melt me like
a siren song.

Consumed by thoughts
to destroy my head.

But tonight's black spots
erased my dread

Reminded me of
all potential.

To overcome the
whether, torrential.

I felt surrounded by
the calming night.

Urging me to not
give up my fight.

Rewritten Tale

Home has never been
where my heart lies,
but where my mind
cries out for at night.

Aren't We All?

Every single setback I have reminded that I am human.

As much as I hate to admit it, that means its okay to fail.

So even when I sour on how this feels so cruel.

My setbacks lead me on my most fulfilling trail.

Together Alone, But Okay.

I visit you again.
So many times I have
watched you stare back at me
until we didn't feel real.
Time didn't feel real.
It was spent so many
times tearing me to pieces
until I was too small to pick back
up and put together. You
may think I hate you, sometimes I do.
But I forgive you. This isn't your fault.
You were there every moment.
You experienced every broken heart,
every anxious album of art,
every promise broken,
everything.
How could I think either one of us
would come out of this whole?
How could I think either one of us
could be strong enough to pull the
other out of this abyss after it was all done?
I was wrong.
We need to do this together.
So I forgive you, and I love you.
No matter what you tell me later
when the meteor creates craters,
I love you, and now I know you love me too.

When We're Awake At Night

When we're awake at night, who are we really? I have thought about this question for so long. The answers always seem to be endless.

The night is such an intriguing time of our lives, and often undervalued one. All of the time that passes, most of it likely spent sleeping. Dreaming of things we would wish would happen. Finding love, happiness, self acceptance and true bliss. A world where no problems arise and each day seems to be solved. Everyone loves everyone, and each day is just moments of everyone experiencing these blissful blessings.

Then there is the nightmares. All of the things I seem to fear the most. The unknown, death, failure, heartbreak, and all of my demons that I push away each day just to get by until the next visit me. Taunting me. Reminding me that no matter how much I try and avoid the fact that they are real, there is no true escape from them. Leaving me awake at night, wondering how I can overcome, how can I survive this.

Sitting in my bed, I try and process everything that just happened. None of it was ever real, you're okay. But am I? A million questions will pass through your mind. Are any of us really okay? How could any of us truly know? What are our reference points? Comparisons of other people? How could we truly know if they are okay based off a picture on a screen? They look so happy. Are they going through anything I am? Am I normal? Is anyone normal?

This is when every insecurity will flow to the shore as a morning wave. All of the times I stared into my mirror and saw all of the flaws that maybe no one else even notices. But to me they are as obvious as the difference between water and concrete. All of the moments spent analyzing my smile, my voice, my hair, my body, and more important than anything: my worth. Spending all this time deciding if it is something that even exists.

Furthermore, wondering if all of the memories I ever made we're spent with people analyzing all of my flaws. Thinking back on every sentence ever said, every smile given, every laugh ever bellowed, every moment ever spent, wondering if it was genuine. Consumed by the fact that all of the memories I ever made could have been my biggest embarrassments and I might never even know. I spend the following moments contemplating everyone I have ever interacted with and their perception of me.

Then the inevitable breakdown. Panic ensues, and all of the next moments are spent floating around my room feeling the purest form of fear I could feel. Palms and underarms perspire. Breath becomes rapid, and a mind moves at the speed of light causing dizziness that sends me to my knees clawing to my bed for some form of comfort to try and combat these psychological and physiological tortures. Long inhales, and heavy exhales. Repeated over and over again. Just enough to halt a collapse. I yearn to leave this space, throw on a pair of shoes, and head out into the darkness of the night.

Here I am left with the calming stillness of our world. In this moment, I am reminded of the endless possibilities that seem to lie before us each day.

The darkness at many moments is meant to send chills down spines of anyone who comes across its path. But in this moment I seem to find myself. A realization that each night we experience our fears, insecurities, sadness, stresses, and breakdowns.

However, we are also able to watch all of this pass. Taken away each night by the shadows, and what's left over is our true selves.

The idea of being consumed by our darkness seems to be spread around consistently. Darkness is what consumes us. It takes a hold of us, swallows us, and spits us out lesser of a person than we ever were before. This is wrong. We can learn from our stillness, our shadows, our darkness. Embrace it, and overcome it. In this way, we control it and become our best selves.

About the Author

Levi Laws has grown up in the Salem, Oregon a majority of his life, and currently lives in Monmouth Oregon. He is a current student at Western Oregon University to graduate in June 2022. He is majoring in education, with a goal of becoming a High School English Teacher. While writing is one of his biggest passions, he also spends his free time painting, going on hikes, reading, coaching youth basketball, and being an AVID tutor at a local high school in his town.

"When We're Awake At Night" is Levi's first published book
Socials:
Instagram: Levilaws_
Twitter: Levilaws__

Business email: Laws_Levi@yahoo.com

Special Thanks

There are so many people I could thank for getting me to this accomplishment. So to not leave any off here is a list, I: am so incredibly grateful for you all, and all of the experiences with you in my life are apart of the reason I am where I am now. Thank you!

All of my family.
Joseph
David
Colton
Kelsey
Caylea
Bekah
Landrey
Leah
Consi
B.J.
Bucholz
Kelsey
Marshall
Paris
T.
A.
J.
A.

Special Shout out

An incredibly talented young artist on the rise, and an amazing young woman, Indika Roseler, who did the cover art. Follow her artistic journey at:

Instagram: indika876

Who Do You Become When You're Awake At Night?

Send your answers to wwaanbook@gmail.com

And lastly, if you need to be reminded today...

BLACK LIVES MATTER and all lives matter is racist rhetoric
BLACK LIVES MATTER and all lives matter is racist rhetoric
BLACK LIVES MATTER and all lives matter is racist rhetoric
BLACK LIVES MATTER and all lives matter is racist rhetoric
BLACK LIVES MATTER and all lives matter is racist rhetoric
BLACK LIVES MATTER and all lives matter is racist rhetoric
BLACK LIVES MATTER and all lives matter is racist rhetoric
BLACK LIVES MATTER and all lives matter is racist rhetoric
BLACK LIVES MATTER and all lives matter is racist rhetoric
BLACK LIVES MATTER and all lives matter is racist rhetoric
BLACK LIVES MATTER and all lives matter is racist rhetoric
BLACK LIVES MATTER and all lives matter is racist rhetoric
BLACK LIVES MATTER and all lives matter is racist rhetoric
BLACK LIVES MATTER and all lives matter is racist rhetoric
BLACK LIVES MATTER and all lives matter is racist rhetoric
BLACK LIVES MATTER and all lives matter is racist rhetoric
BLACK LIVES MATTER and all lives matter is racist rhetoric
BLACK LIVES MATTER and all lives matter is racist rhetoric
BLACK LIVES MATTER and all lives matter is racist rhetoric
BLACK LIVES MATTER and all lives matter is racist rhetoric
BLACK LIVES MATTER and all lives matter is racist rhetoric
BLACK LIVES MATTER and all lives matter is racist rhetoric
BLACK LIVES MATTER and all lives matter is racist rhetoric
BLACK LIVES MATTER and all lives matter is racist rhetoric
BLACK LIVES MATTER and all lives matter is racist rhetoric